Just Designs

by
Meriah Smith

Also written by Meriah Smith:

Eden Symbiotic

Unexpected Cargo

To see more art by the author visit:

www.cherokeegal1975.deviantart.com

How to use this book:

This book is a desgin idea book for your use. These designsfeatured in my book are made to decorate anything you desire to have them stamped, stiched, drawn or printed on.

How you can use them is simple. Just place them on a scanner to copy the pictures and with a tiny bit of editing to trim the edges, you can place them on stationary or cards. You can also print them out on thin paper to use as a needle point pattern guide on apparel and anything else you would like to see them on.

Like tattoos or body paint? Bring this book with you to show the artist what you are inerested in having painted or inked into your skin.

Need a decorating idea for your home? My paterns would look great on pillows, tiles, wallpaper, or any other item at home you would like to decorate.

The posiblities are endless!

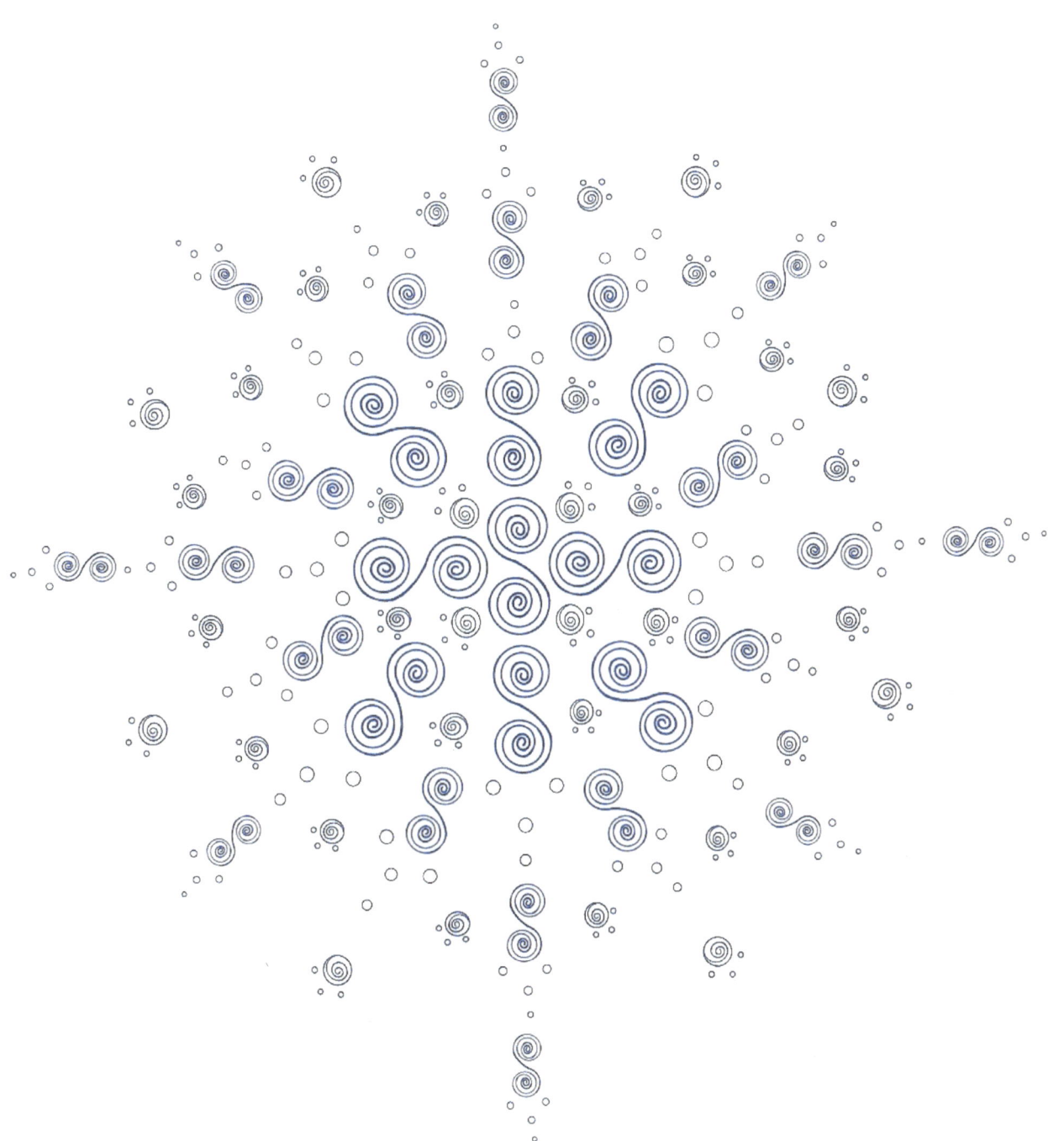

Blue Ink

Like most of my designs, this one started out as a random doodle on a piece of scratch paper I was using to record phone numbers and other bits of information. Originally done in blue ballpoint pen, I later refined this design using my computer graphics program. Unable to think of a better name for it, I just call this one Blue Ink.

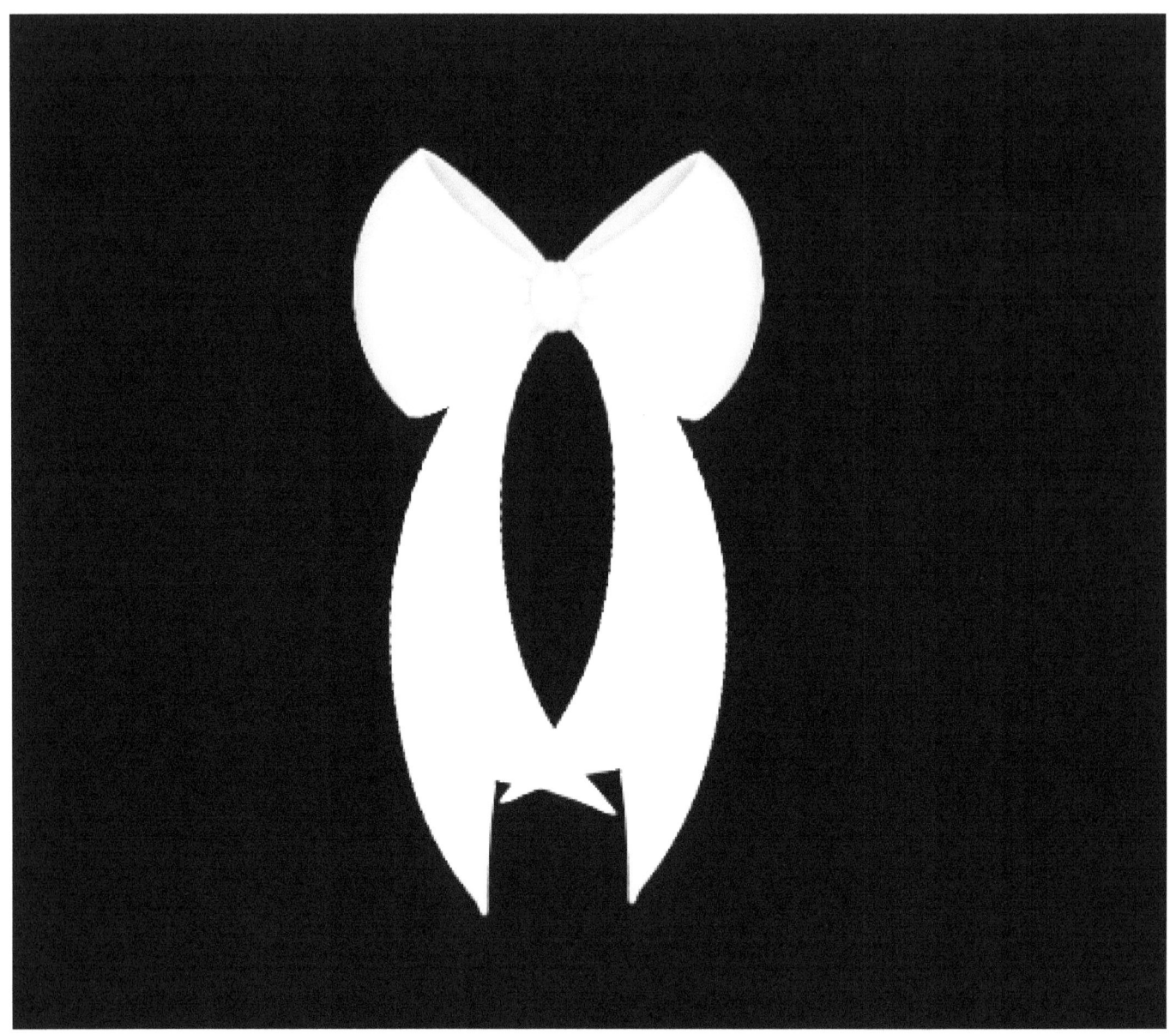

Bow Element:

Above: This design is something I created to be used again and again on my book cover designs. In my graphics program I can create layers and I kept the back ground and the bow separate. That way I could copy and paste the premade bow so I wouldn't have to draw it again from scratch every time I wanted to use a bow. Might make a nice t-shirt design or a card design.

Busy Tile Pattern:

Page right: This pattern started is another one of my doodles that I refined. The disks on this design are all supposed to be shinny metallic gold and it is actually sideways so it will fit on the page better. But really, it doesn't have a right side up, so it doesn't really matter. This one can be placed on any wide area, especially tiles and wallpaper, but it also might look good on a skirt, quilt or a couch. Or it might look nice on a piece of stationary, copied and faded out so they type can be seen clearly.

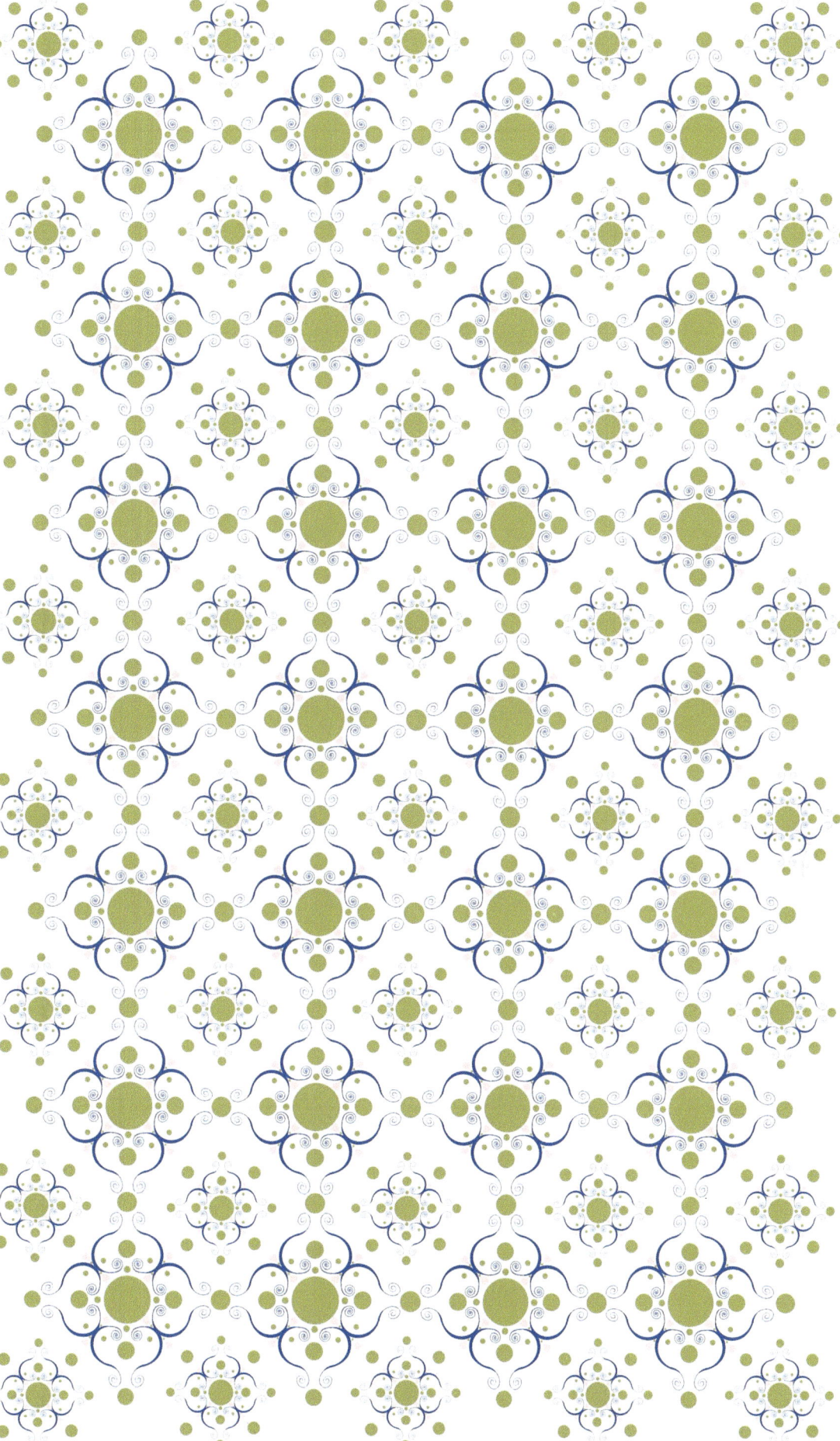

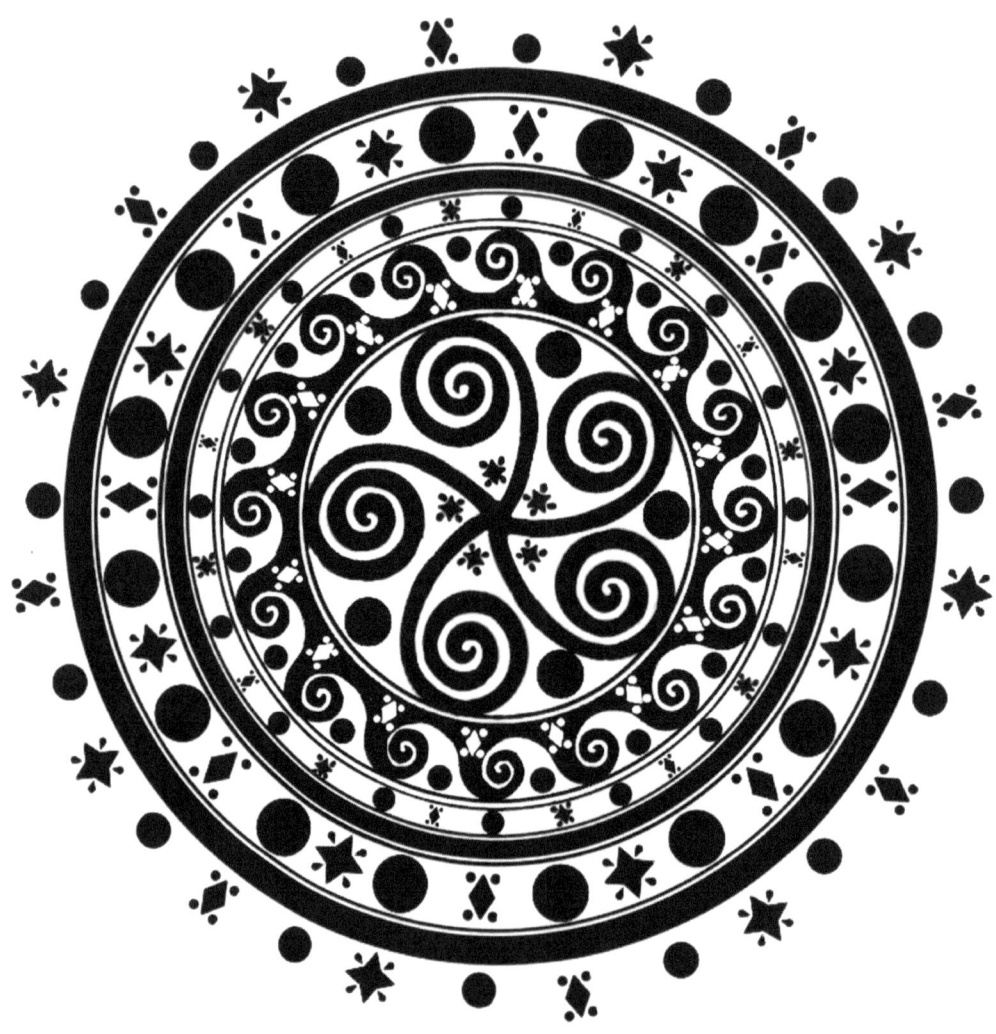

Celesial Wind Whorl

   Originally another doodle that I later refined on a piece of Strathmore drawing paper in black Sharpie marker, then later did a colored version in colored pencil. When I received my graphics program from my father as a gift, I used it to recreate my designs in digital. The shape tools I had available to me and the ability to copy and paste repeating elements of my design made the whole process of creation much easier and more consistent in form than I could ever done by hand. If you wish to see my original versions done by hand, just visit my site listed on the first page of thsi book and check out my Abstract Dump folder. They will be on page four.

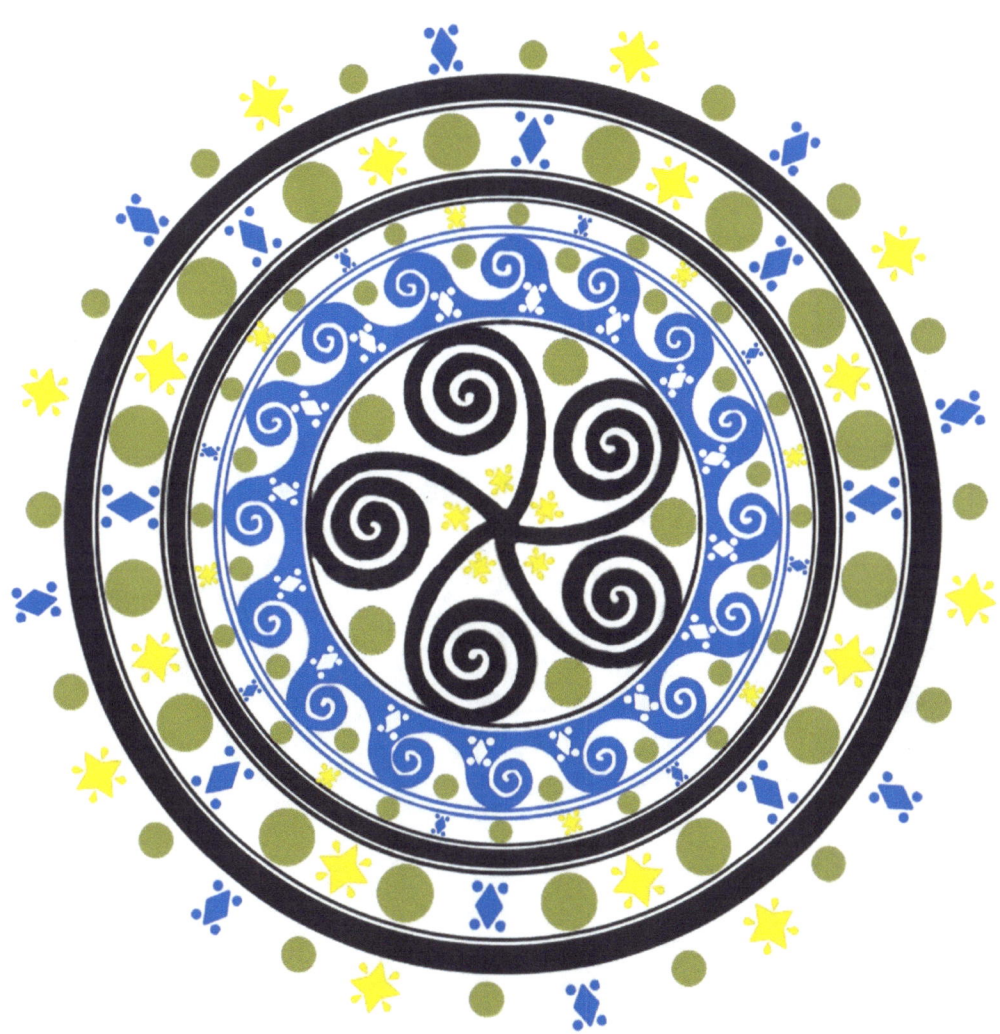

Celestial Wind Whorl

This is a digital version of the colored design. The circles are all supposed to be shinny gold. I also used this same one to create the other three version of my design for the sake of creating color variations. This one is the first one of this design that I did in digital. Later with a bit of experimenting I was able to create the black and white version on the opposite page, closely mimicking the original drawing done in Sharpie.

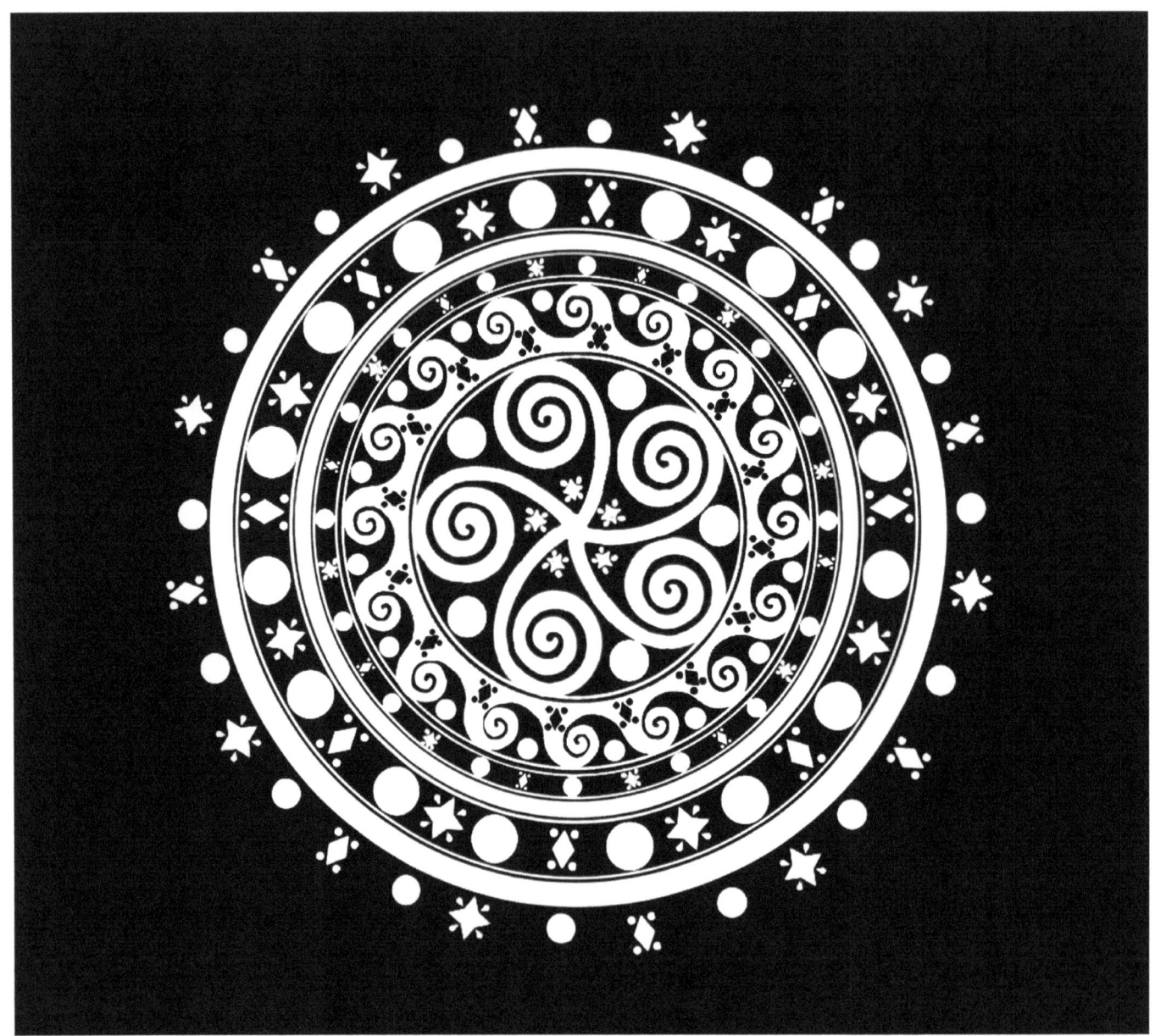

Clestial Wind Whorl Negative

This is merely my black and white version of my design inverted. I have a function on my graphics program that allows me to do this.

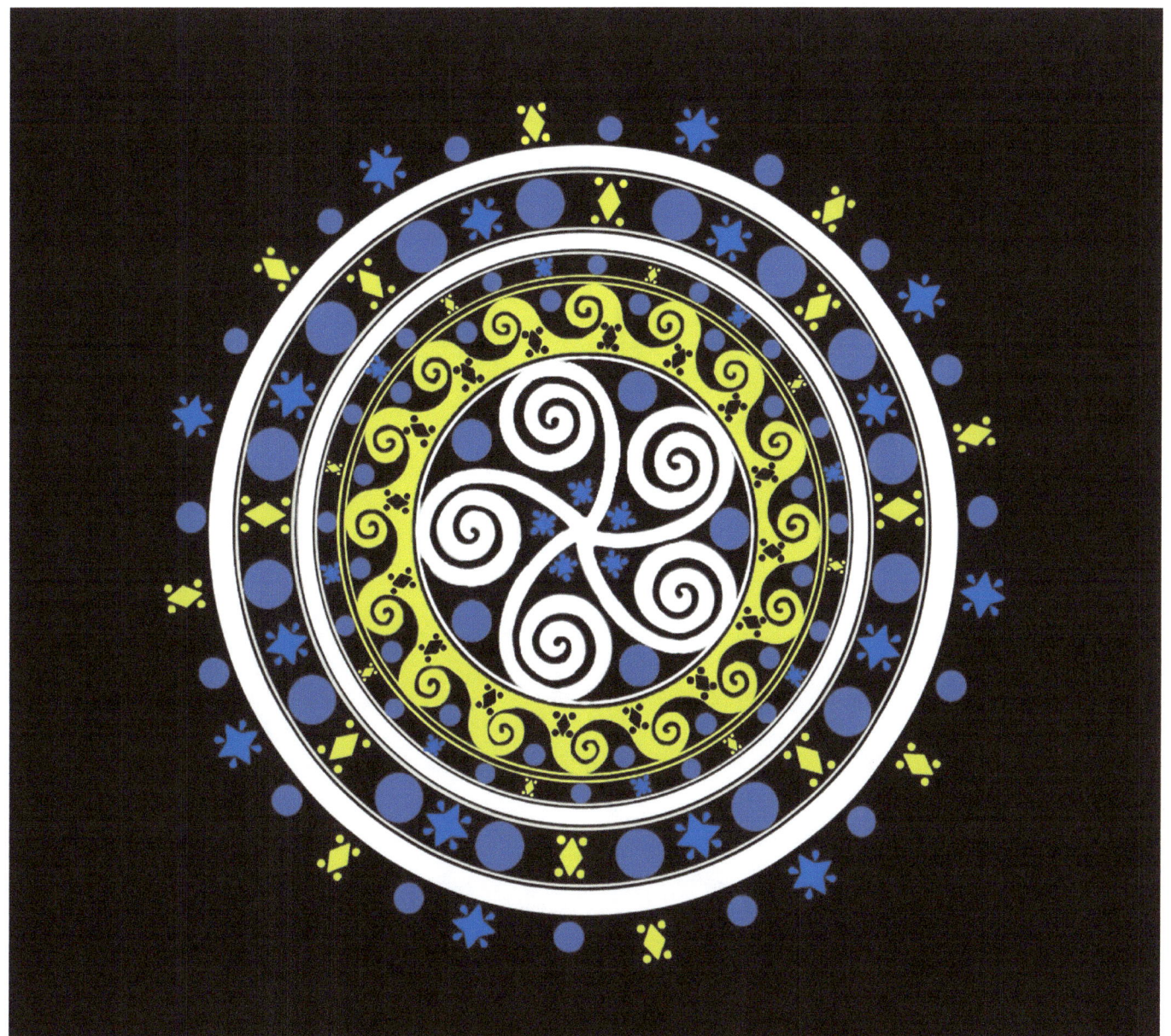

Celestial Wind Whorl Inverted

An experiment that went wrong. I was trying to create a black and white verson of this design by simply using the reverse color funtion on my graphics program. It didn't work, but the end result is beautiful anyway, so I kept it. The gold here is supposed to be shiny, but I don't know how to express that in a flat design. Maybe if you had a paint pen and some shape tools you could draw in the metalic colors as a fun coloring project.

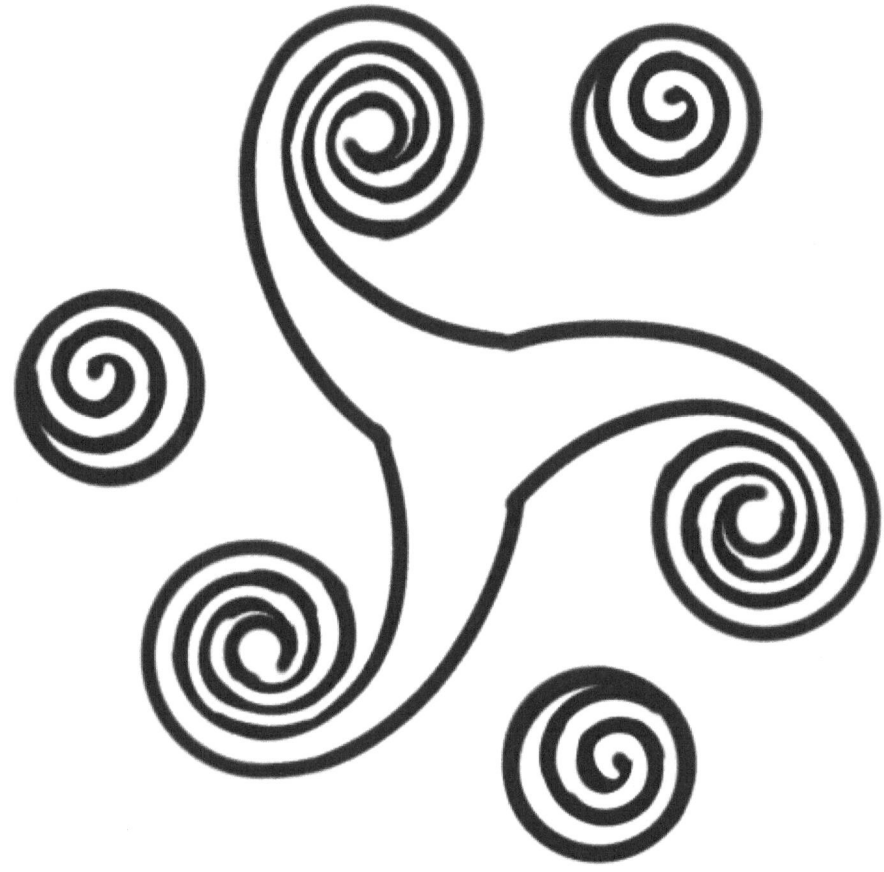

Cloud Whorl

It may look black here, but it is really a very dark indigo blue. This one is one of the few designs that I have created that didn't start out as a random doodle. I was watching a video of the Earth from space on Facebook when I happened to see three whorling storm systems come together and make a pattern very similar to this one. Eventually, I copied it and embelished it a little.

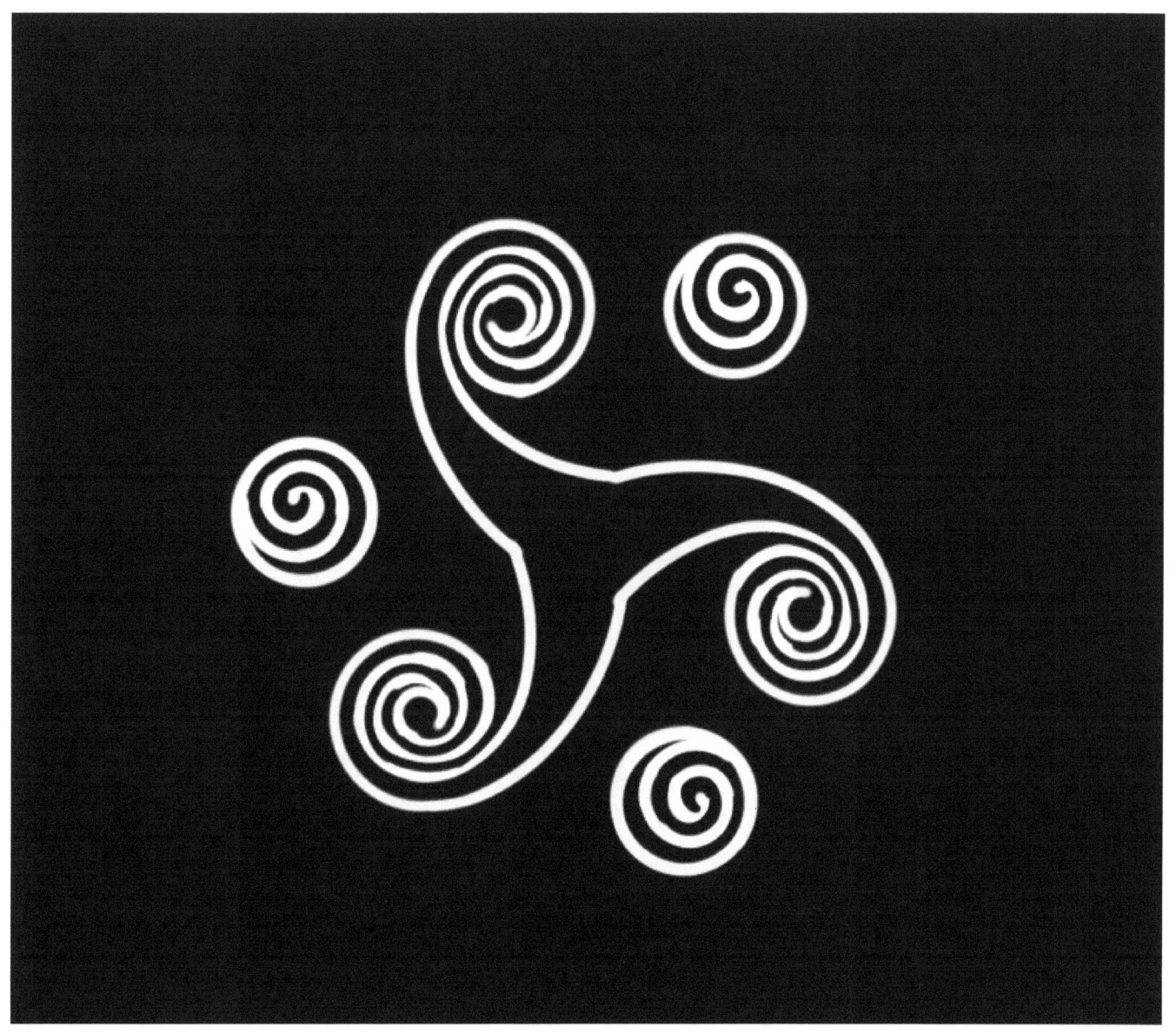

Cloud Whorl Inverted

Same pattern, just inverted and colored black and white.

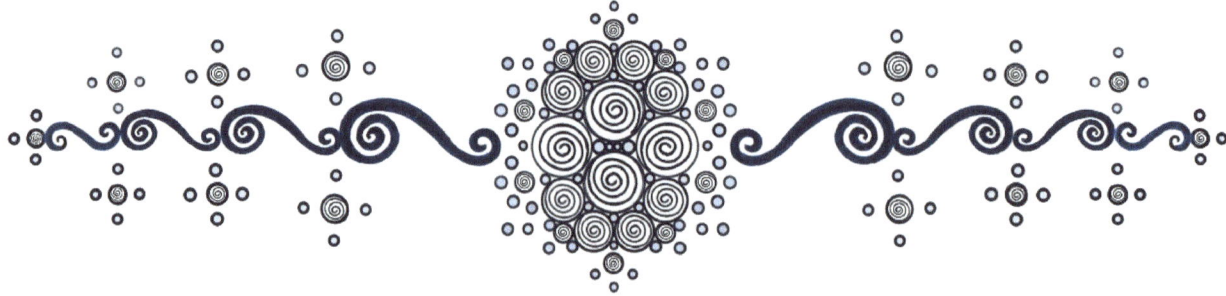

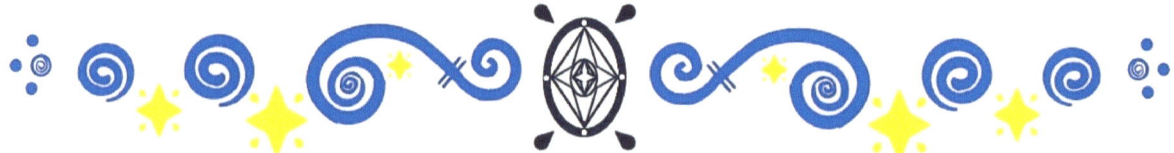

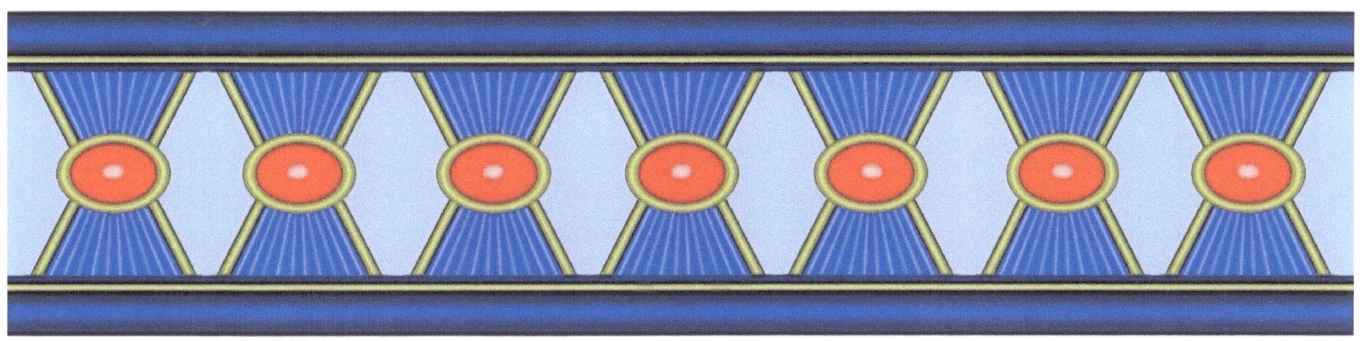

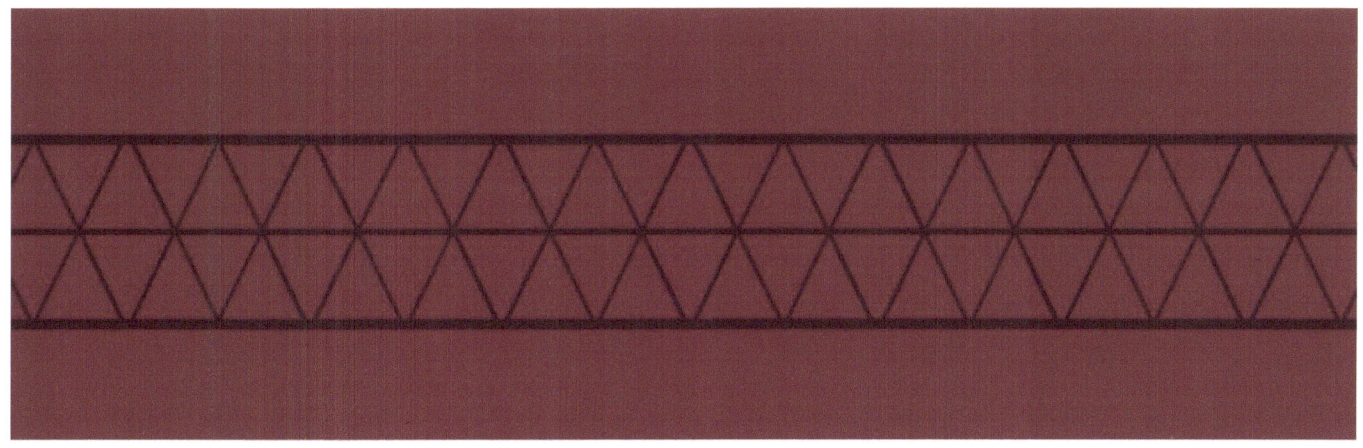

See next page:

Previous Pages:

Wing Design

Above Left: My very first abstract design I have ever created. Originally a doodle in my anatomy text book, it was inspired by frustrated boredom. Later I recorded it as a sort of rough scribble on another piece of paper, then refined it using colored pencils. Eventually I did it digitally. The center part where it is grey is supposed to be shining silver.

Psychedelic Whee!

Middle left: This is one of my more difficult designs to create and I would not have been able to complete it without the help of my graphics program. Originally I had done this in sketch by hand and later I attempted to color it. Unfortunately, I did accidently messed it up and I was not able to correct the problem until now.

Diamond Star Whorl

Bottom Left: Third in the series you see here on the opposite page, this one had also began as a hand drawn sketch. But yet again I had trouble coloring it and seriously messed it up. Fortunately I was able to do it again digitally and finally was able to get it just right.

Egyptian Pattern

Above right I actually found this pattern on a front cover of an Archeology magazine. There was a wall relief featuring Egyptian glyphs and drawings. What caught my eye was the border above and below the work. I liked it and I was thinking something like a pattern for a bead bracelet. So I recorded it and admittedly embellished it a bit. Originally the red was a terra cotta color and there was no metallic gold leaf placed in the design.

The First Art

Middle left: I found a similar pattern on a documentary about the origin of abstract thinking in humans and the possible connection of expressing that kind of thought through art. This pattern was discovered in one of the very oldest archeological sites ever discovered in Africa and had originally been done a bit crudely on a chunk of ocher flattened on one side and carved into it. I copied it in digital and refined it, keeping the original colors of the art itself.

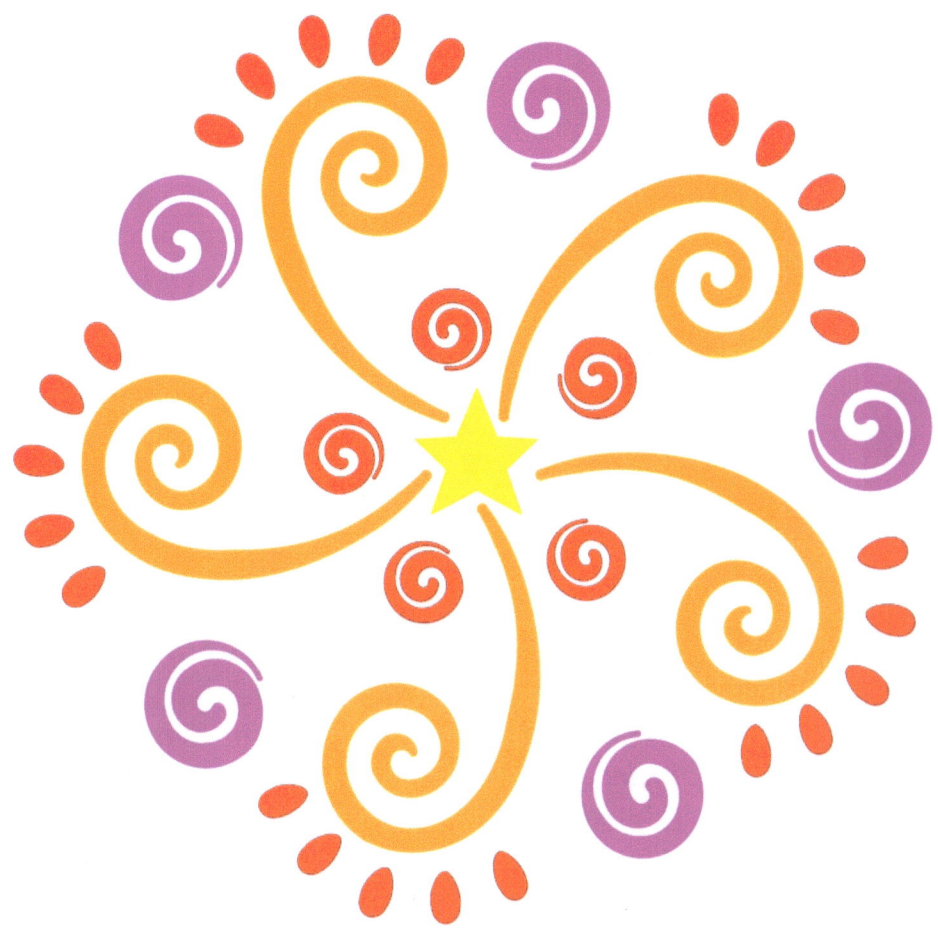

Geo-Works

Originally a hand drawn doodle, I refined this one and gave it hot colors of fire. This pattern reminds me of an abstract firework. The first completed version was done in Prismacolor marker and this one has been done in digital.

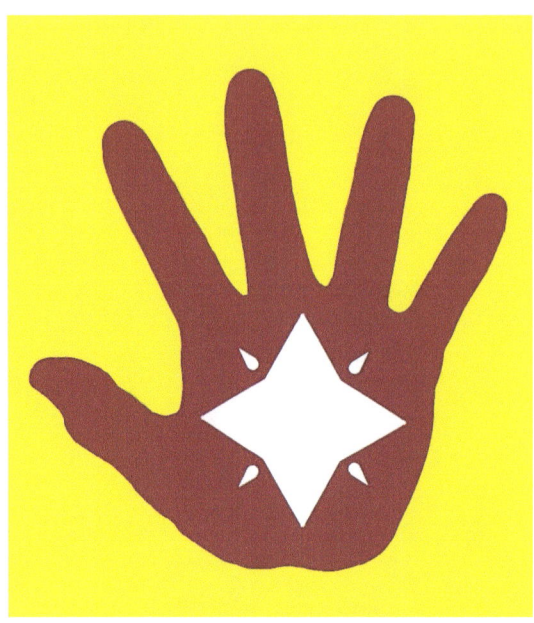

The Hand and Star

Above: A design that I originally did when I was high school. It just popped into my head one day and I drew it in colored pencil. The original was quite rough, so eventually I did a more refined version using my own right hand as a stencil and using my left hand with a bit of difficulty to trace it. That version is currently hanging on my bedroom wall. Later I did another version in marker that looked even better and I used that version to help me make the digital version you see here. I actually used this design in my novel Eden Symbiotic on the front cover art and also as a line design to decorate the front cover page and at the end of my chapters when there was space for it.

Hands

Below: Just me fooling around with my graphics program. It is actually my Hand and Star design done twice in the same picture, with one flipped over in the opposite direction.

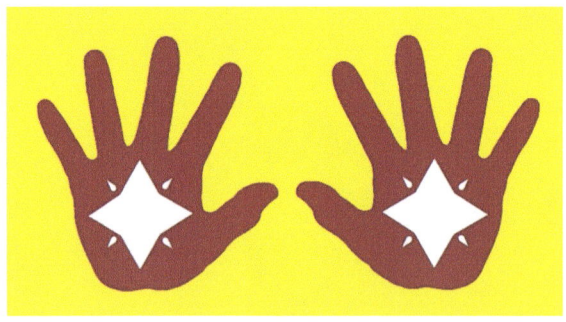

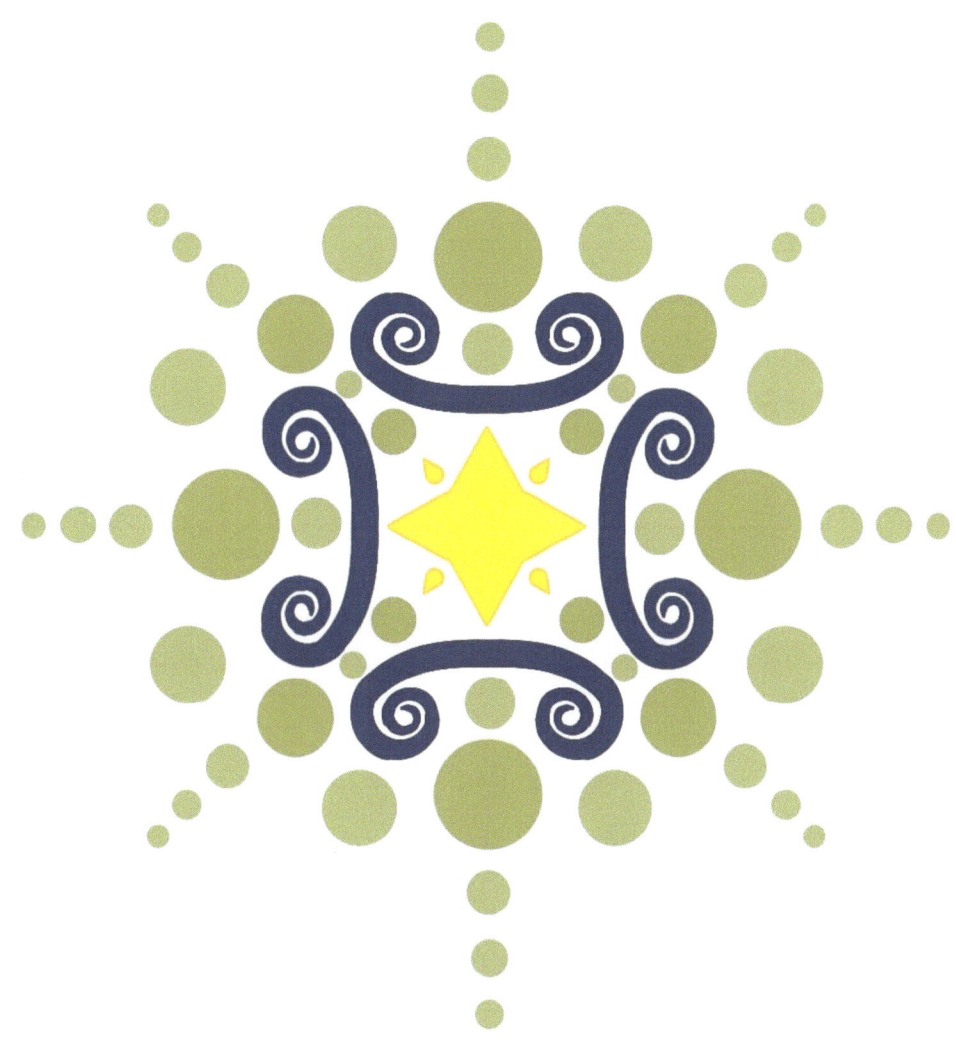

Star Burst

This design started out as a vague idea in my head that I did a quick sketch in ballpoint pen on line paper. It stayed a rough sketch for quite a few years and it wasn't until I received my graphics program I finally got around to drawing it. The circles here are supposed to be shinny metallic gold.

Heart Design

This design started out as a random doodle. Can be used for chairs, t-shirts...anything.

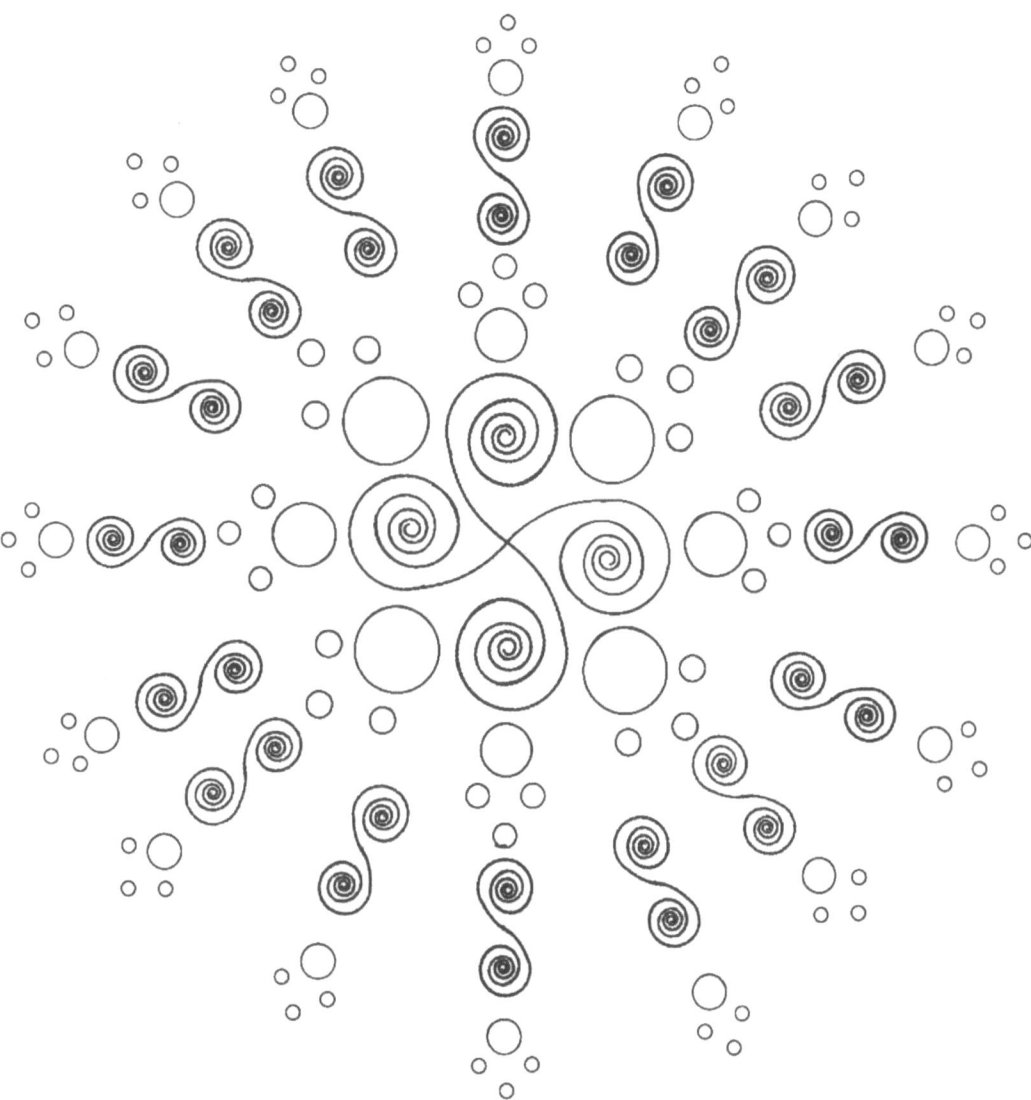

Lines and Circles

This one had always been digital. I actually finished it in about an hour early one morning.

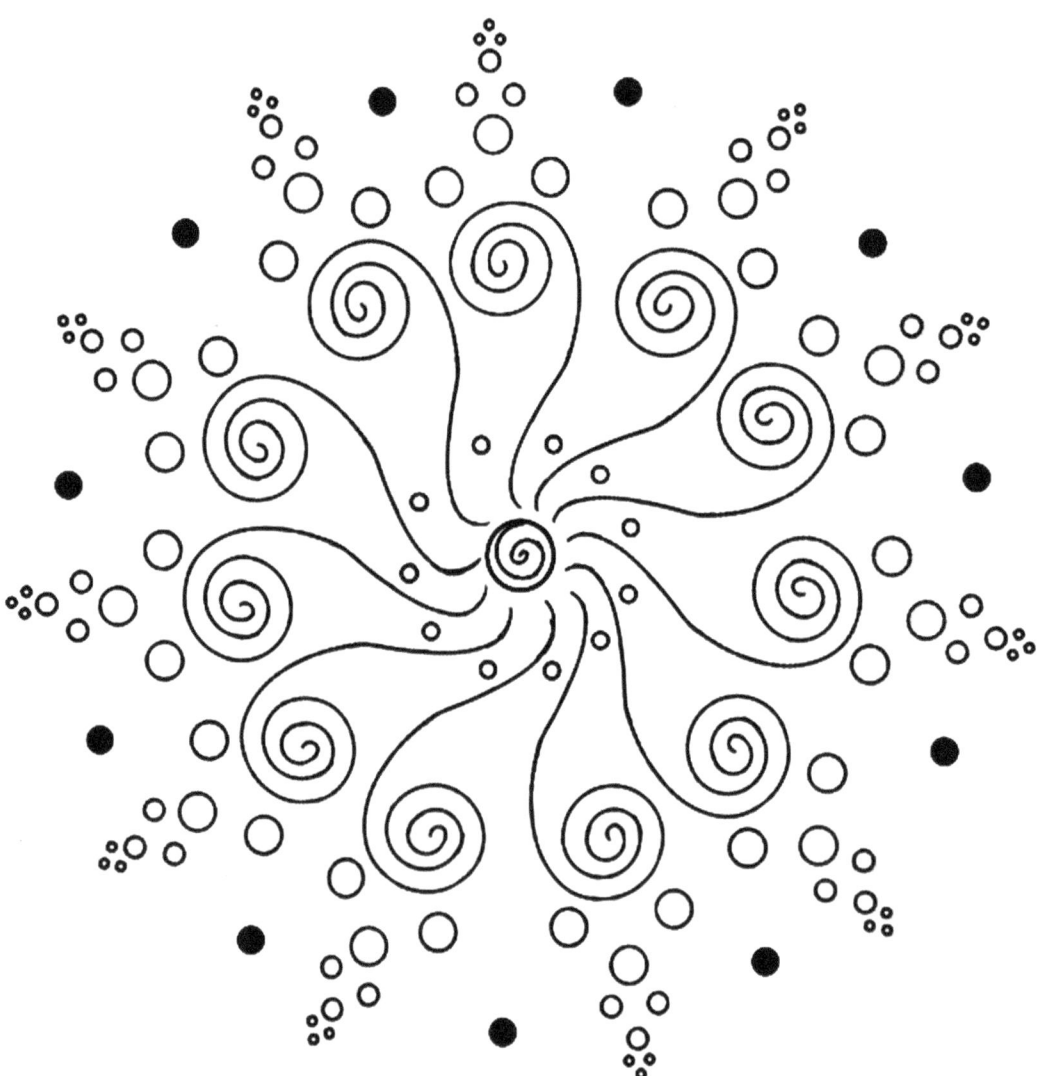

Line Flower

Another doodle I refined. I actually used this one as a decorative illustration in my novel Unexpected Cargo for the cover page and at the end of each chapter when there was a blank space big enough for it to be there.

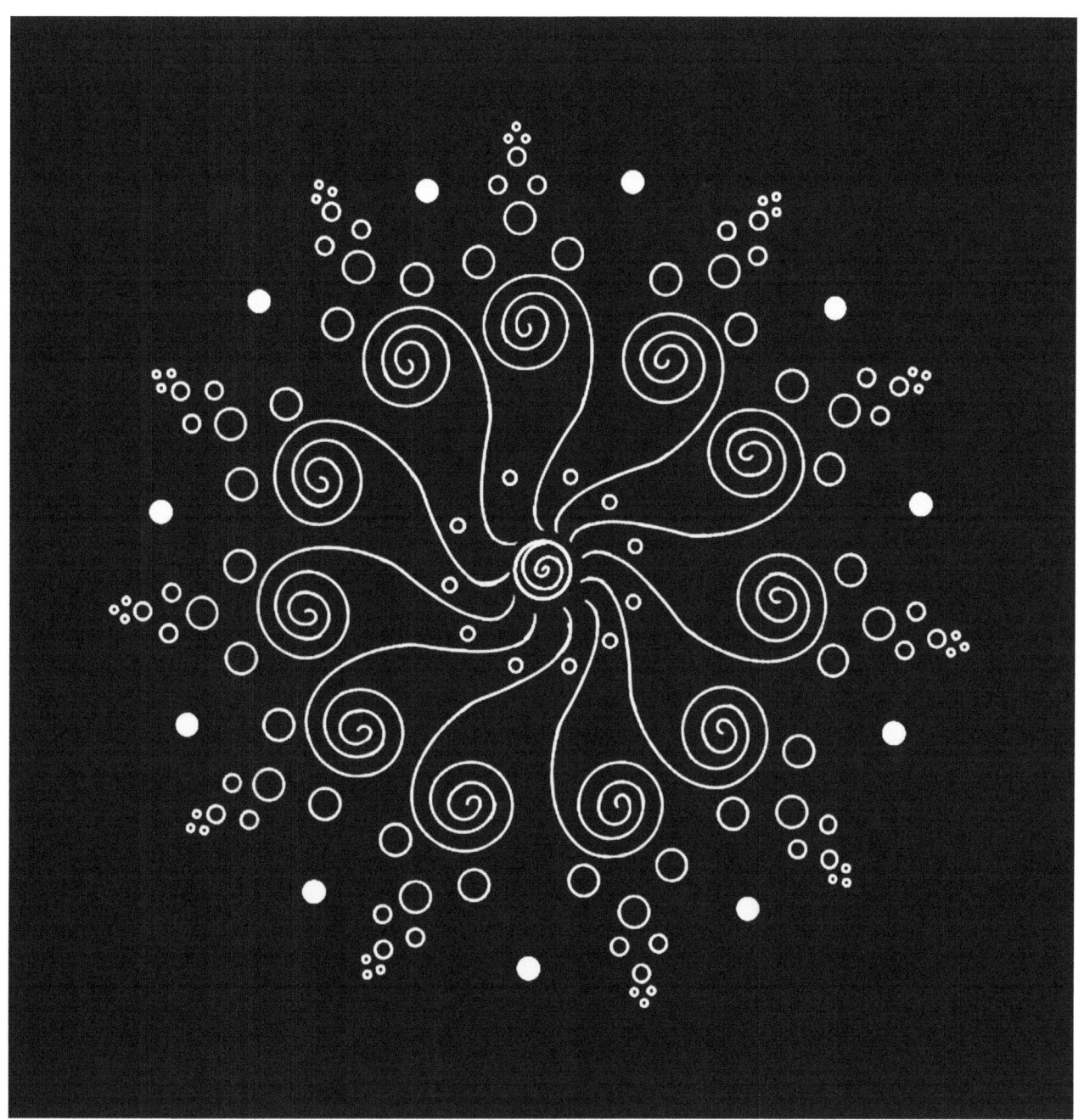

Line Flower Negative

Same design as the opposite page, just with its colors inverted.

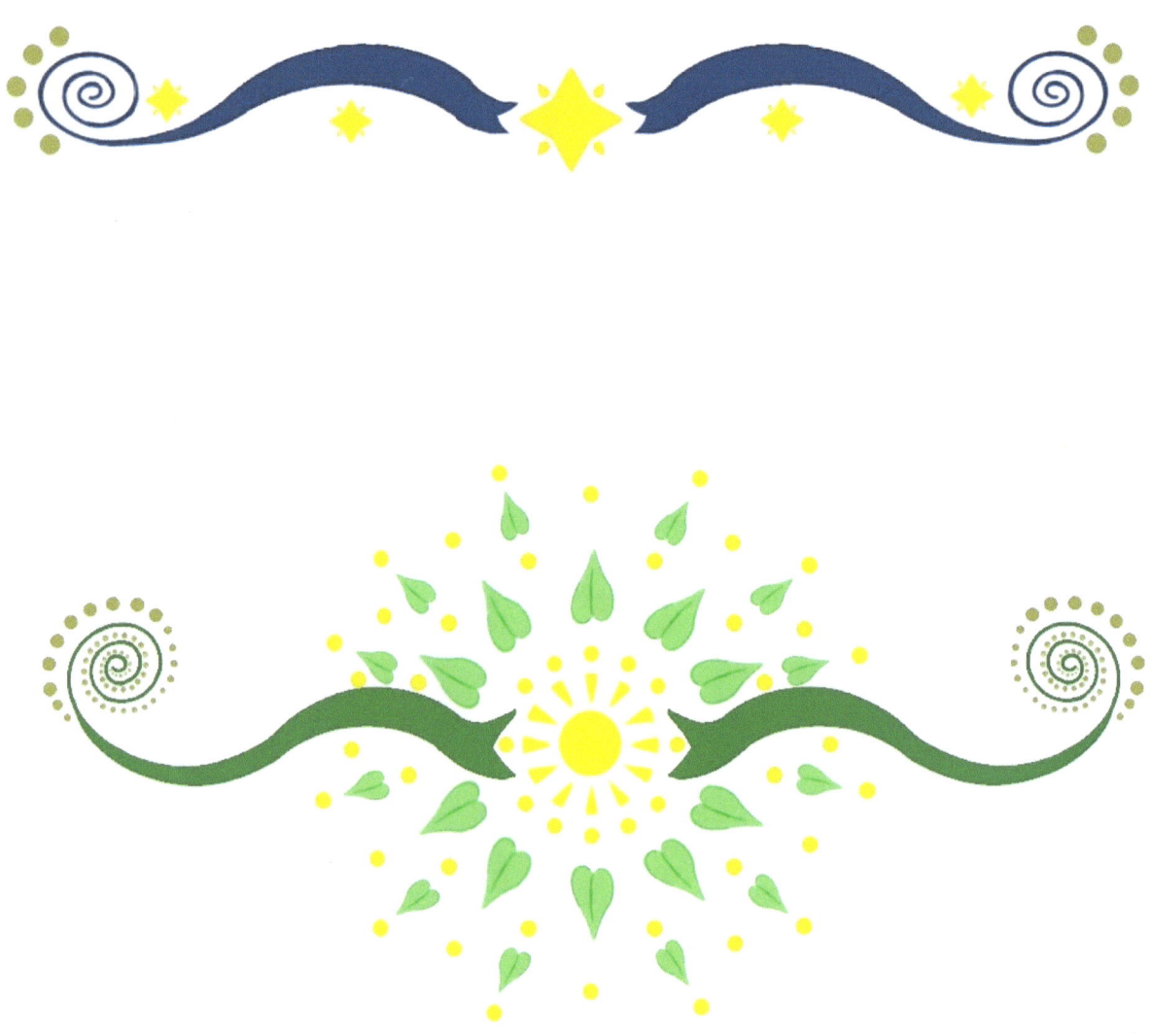

Stars and Ribbons

Above: Another doodle that I later refined in digital. The circles at the ends are supposed to be shinny gold. One person online mentioned that it could be used as fantasy makeup over the eyebrows...an interesting idea.

Sunflower

Bottom: I created this one on the same day as Stars and Ribbons. A random scrawl on paper that I refined with my graphics program. The dots are supposed to be metallic gold.

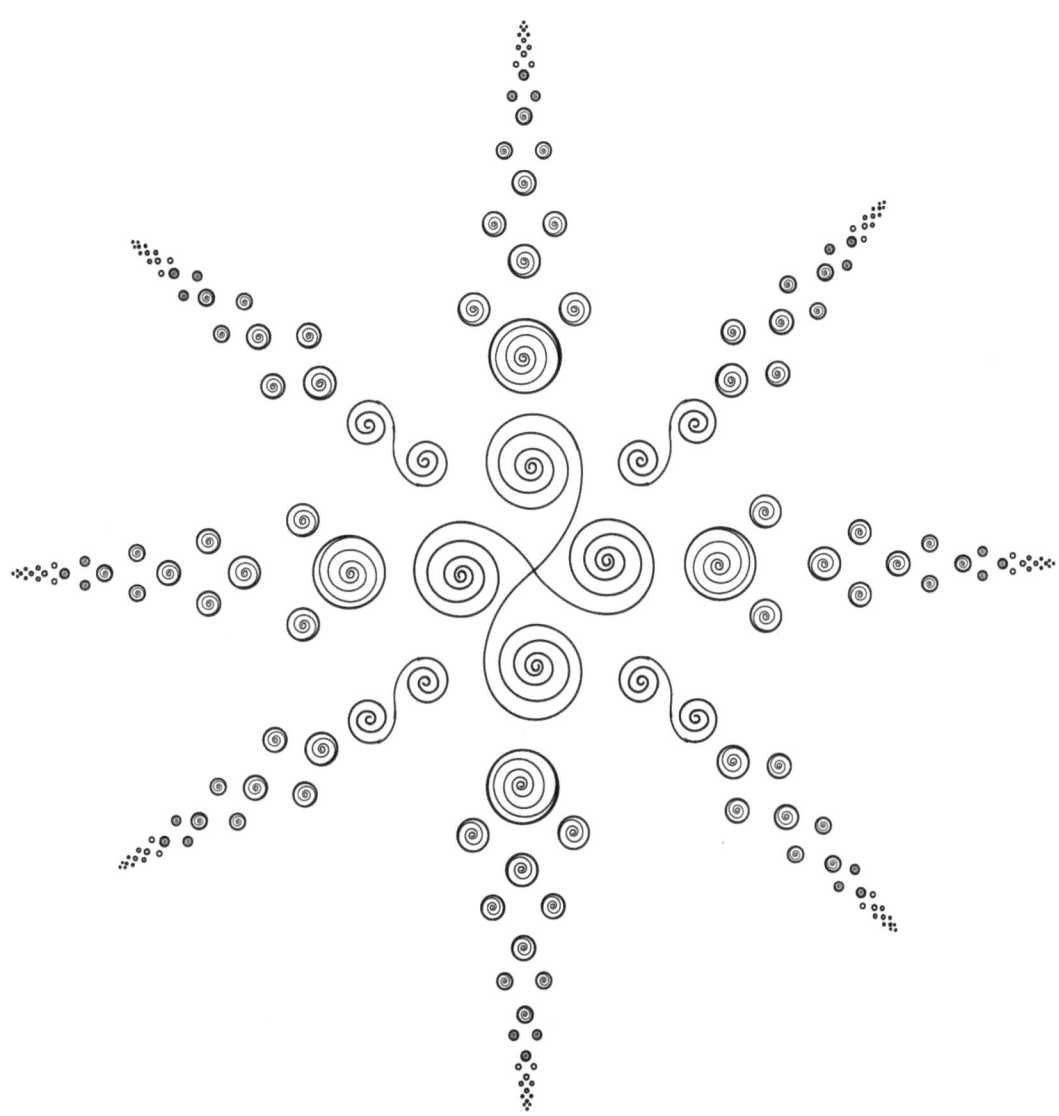

Whorl Design

Originally a hand drawn pencil sketch that I tried to color and promptly messed up. I scanned it and attempted to enhance it with MS Paint with some success. When I got my graphics program I used the original sketch as a template and drew it in this refined digital version.

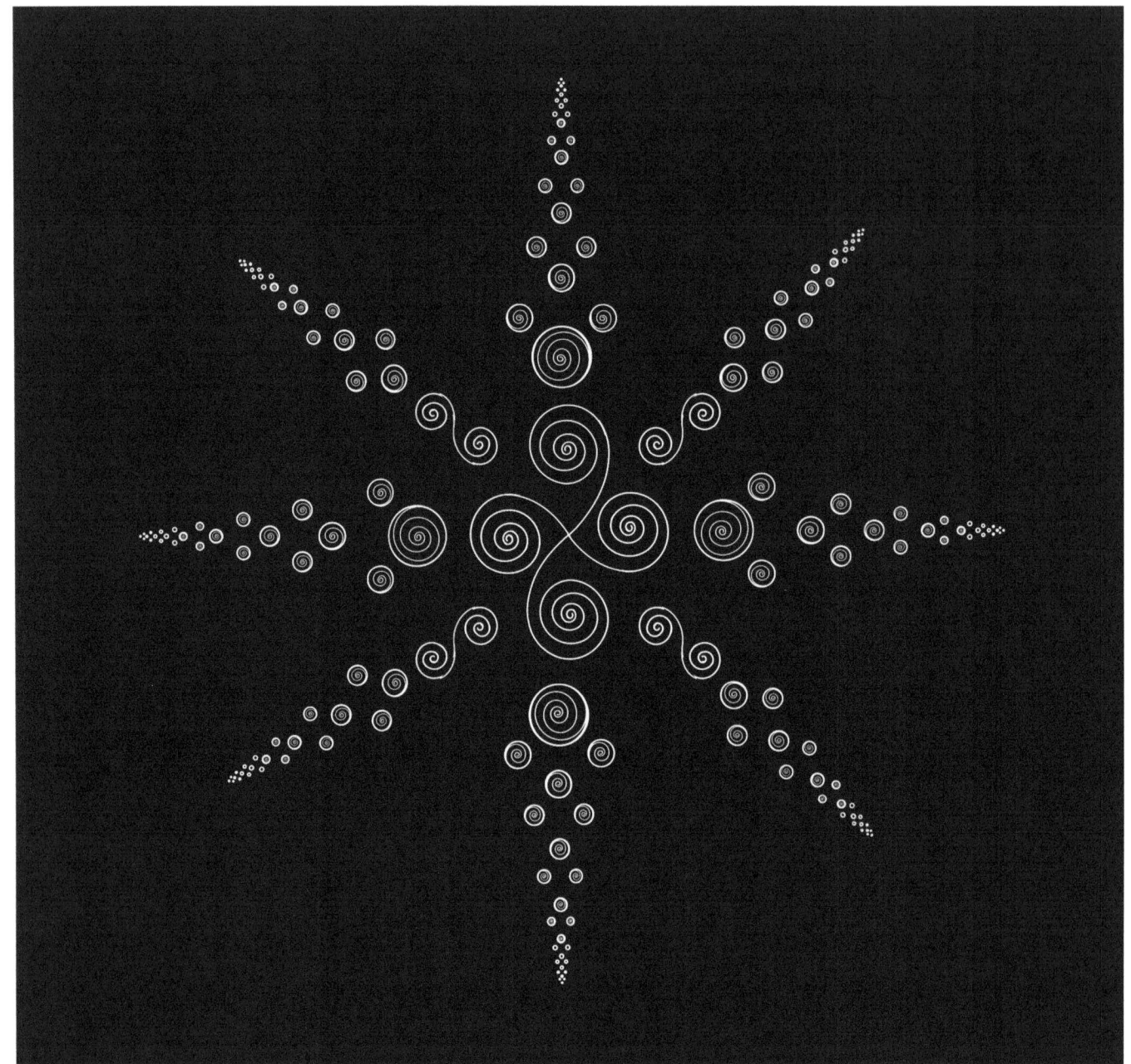

Whorl Design Negative

Same as the Whorl Design, just with its colors inverted.

www.ingramcontent.com/pod-product-compliance
Lightning Source LLC
Chambersburg PA
CBHW050430180526
45159CB00005B/2477